Styling Material UI Components

Syntax, APIs, and Detailed Examples

Introduction

Material-UI is an excellent library used to make countless web UIs look slick and professional. In my time of using Material-UI, I have been impressed by its power and ubiquity. I have also encountered challenges in styling my components precisely as I desired. I created this book to aid others in their use of Material-UI and to speed up their development times.

About the Author

I earned my Master of Science in Information Systems in 2012 and have been a software engineer at Fortune 500 companies since then. I enjoy teaching other developers and creating software-related businesses.

Chapter 1: JSS Selector Pattern Overview

To efficiently style components in Material-UI, first you need to understand what styling libraries and rules Material-UI follows. Material-UI uses JSS, also known as CSS-in-JS. In plain English, JSS takes CSS syntax and converts is to JavaScript so that you can write your CSS in JavaScript.

This implies that you can take knowledge of CSS syntax and readily apply it to JSS and styling of your Material-UI components. Let's take a look at a few examples of the syntax. If you are already familiar with JSS and simply want some Material-UI examples, jump to Chapter 2.

General rules:

- JSS uses camel-case instead of dashes (i.e. fontWeight instead of font-weight)
- There is no '.' in front of class names (i.e. buyButton instead of .buyButton)
- Imports and other variables are fine. Remember, this is JavaScript
- Other JavaScript syntax is fine (i.e. object destructuring)

Pseudo-class selectors:

Example 1.
Here we select an element with class buyButton when it is hovered over.

```
buyButton: {
  backgroundColor: 'blue',
  fontSize: 24,
  '&:hover': {
    border: '4px solid red',
    cursor: 'pointer'
  }
}
```

As a reminder, the '&' is a reference to the parent selector when nesting. So '&:hover' is really buyButton:hover.

Example 2.
Here we have an example of two pseudo-classes being applied to the same element. Notice that there are no spaces in the double pseudo-class selector.

```
personChecker: {
  '&:checked:disabled': {
    width: 20,
    height: 20
  }
}
```

If you want to see more like this, here's another example from the JSS docs: https://cssinjs.org/react-todo-mvc/. The github for the example code is https://github.com/cssinjs/react-todomvc-jss/blob/master/client/components/MainSection/style.js

Example 3.
Take a look at nested pseudo-class syntax:

```
buyButton: {
  '&:hover': {
    backgroundColor: 'blue',
    '&:before: {
      textDecoration: 'bold',
    }
  }
}
```

This will select an element that is hovered and has the :before pseudo-class applied. This syntax allows you to have certain styles always applied on :hover (backgroundColor, in this case), and only some styles applied on both :hover *and* :before.

Child Selectors:

The syntax for selecting child elements or classes is similar to selecting pseudo-classes. Notice the '& span' syntax (a space because it's a child).

```
form: {
  "& span": {
    backgroundColor: "red",
    margin: 4
  }
}
```

This will select all span elements that are children of elements with form class applied. Note that form is a class name here, not an element selector.

With these rules and examples, we should be able to read and understand JSS code that we see used in the styling of Material-UI components. However, we still need to understand the rules that Material-UI uses to apply classes to an object. This will be discussed in the next chapter.

Helpful Resources:
- The JSS docs: https://cssinjs.org/?v=v10.3.0
- A CodeSandbox with the examples above: https://codesandbox.io/s/jss-pseudo-class-selectors-nnlty

Chapter 2: Customizing Components the Material-UI Way

There are three primary techniques for styling Material-UI (MUI) components. Each one is more powerful than the previous, but also requires more code. Having all three tools in your toolbelt will enable you to overcome challenges with styling and speed your development time.

I will include a github gist that contains all the code snippets below. However, the gist has better formatting than I can do in this eBook.

The API is here: https://material-ui.com/customization/components/

Option 1: className

React developers will be familiar with the className property on React Nodes. Material-UI is a React component library, so naturally className is available.

I'll go over a few examples below, but let's skip to the challenge with className and Material-UI: MUI has its own styling "under the hood", and these styles will override className when there is a conflict.

Let's start with a TextField component. Notice that I have given it a class via className.

```
<TextField
  className={classes.customInput}
  variant='outlined'
  disabled
  label='Text Field 1'
/>
```

And here is the customInput class.

```
customInput: {
  margin: 12,
  '&$disabled': {
    borderColor: 'orange'
  }
}
```

And here is the result. Notice that the margin applied, but the border color did not. This is because the *variant: 'outlined'* has a default border color. This means we need to try a more powerful option if we want to successfully style the TextField.

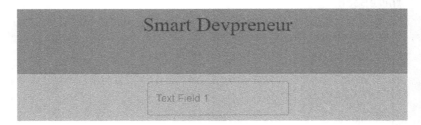

Option 2: classes object property

When className is unable to cut through the default styling on a component, we turn to the classes object property.

Normally, the classes object property is relatively easy to apply. For example, you might have a button with the following classes applied:

```
<Button
  classes={{
    root: classes.root
  }}
/>
```

Some components, such as TextField are more complex components. TextField actually encapsulates an Input component, so you have to target *either* the TextField classes *or* the InputProps classes depending on your goal. Knowing which to target can be a challenge with MUI.

In our TextField example where we tried to style the border color, we actually need to target the InputProps.

```
<TextField
  className={classes.customInput}
  variant='outlined'
  disabled
  label='Text Field 1'
  InputProps={{
    classes: {
      root: classes.root,
      disabled: classes.disabled,
      notchedOutline: classes.notchedOutline
    }
  }}
/>
```

Believe it or not, all three of those classes need to be targeted (root, disabled, and notchedOutline). However, we only need to actually give root the custom styling.

```
root: {
  '&$disabled $notchedOutline': {
    borderColor: 'orange'
  }
},
disabled: {},
notchedOutline: {}
```

The disabled and notchedOutline classes are necessary in the Styles file simply to make the compiler happy.

And there we have it:

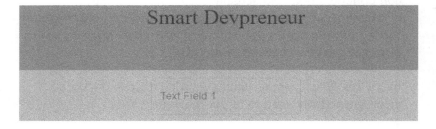

The knowledge and code required to apply the proper styling were a challenging roadblock. This brings us to the third option.

Option 3: Styled Components

This option is far easier and you can use dev tools to uncover what you need to target.

Take a look at the DOM in Dev Tools:

Notice the classes applied and elements created by Material-UI when it rendered TextField: `.MuiOutlinedInput-root`, `.Mui-disabled`, and `fieldset`

We can target these classes and elements with selectors when creating a Styled Component.

Styled Components require the styled-components package from npm. After importing it, you simply create a Styled Component that overrides the original MUI component and immediately includes all styles.

Take a look at the StyledTextField below. The original TextField was overridden with custom styling. Then the StyledTextField is simply used as though it were a TextField, but no classes or classNames are needed. In my experience it is simpler and superior to the classes object.

```
const StyledTextField = styled(TextField)`
  .MuiOutlinedInput-root {
    margin: 12px;
```

```
      &.Mui-disabled fieldset {
        border-color: orange;
      }
      &:hover fieldset {
        border-color: green;
      }
    }
  `;

export const CustomTextField: FC = () => {
  const classes = useStyles();

  return <form className={classes.parentForm}>
    <StyledTextField
      variant='outlined'
      disabled
      label='Text Field 1'
    />
  </form>
}
```

This gives us the same result as using the classes object but far less MUI knowledge is required.

Helpful Resources:
- The source code for the above examples is here: https://gist.github.com/Jon20111/3d6bc73f89ac26d974 76cb2f00a21740
- The class object names (option 2) and global class names (option 3) can be found in the docs here: https://material-ui.com/api/input/#css. This links to the Input props since that's what needed to be targeted for the TextField. TextField is really a wrapper around the Input component. You will need to find the appropriate MUI component and look at its CSS documentation.

Additional Examples

The following examples can all be found in this CodeSandbox:
https://codesandbox.io/s/mui-custom-component-styling-lmzxs. The Dialog and Accordion examples are loosely based on demos from the Material-UI docs.

- **Dialog Component Border:**

Let's start with a relatively simple example of changing the border on a Material-UI Dialog box. The Dialog component is a good candidate for class object styling.

That blue border can be added simply via the classes object:

```
<Dialog
  classes={{
    container: classes.container
  }}
...
/>
```

The container class simply has a blue border style. The class names to target can be found here: https://material-ui.com/api/dialog/

- **Form Control/TextField:**

Here's an interesting example of how to customize a TextField with variant='outlined'. The below TextField has the default border color but the text in the label is grey (default is the same blue as the border).

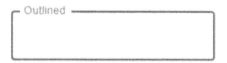

```
//styles
inputLabel: {
  "&.shrink": {
    color: "grey"
  }
}
```

```
//JSX
<TextField
  InputLabelProps={{
    classes: {
      root: classes.inputLabel,
      shrink: "shrink"
    }
  }}
  label="Outlined"
  variant="outlined"
/>
```

I targeted the root and shrink classes using the class object API. Notice in the CodeSandbox that the border color on the FormControl root class doesn't affect the TextField.

- **Button inside FormControl**

Sometimes setting margin inside of a FormControl where margin="dense" can be tricky. However, here is a simple solution:

```
//Styles
root: {
  "& > *": {
    margin: theme.spacing(2),
    borderColor: theme.status.danger
  }
}

//JSX
<FormControl
  margin="dense"
  classes={{
    root: classes.root
  }}
>
  <Button variant="outlined">Click Me</Button>
</FormControl>
```

This method mixes typical css selectors with the classes object API. I'll discuss the theme.status.danger syntax in the next chapter.

- **Custom Divider**

It's hard to show a screenshot of a custom Divider. However, if you run the CodeSandbox mentioned at the top of this section, you will see a custom Divider called StyledDivider. It simply has a little extra margin-top and margin-bottom.

```
const StyledDivider = styled(Divider)`
  &.MuiDivider-root {
    margin-top: 8px;
    margin-bottom: 8px;
  }
`;
```

I can't emphasize enough the need for attention to detail when adding custom styling to these components. Notice in the StyledDivider that there are no quotation marks around the values for margin-top or margin-bottom. If you add quotation marks the browser will literally try to add them to the css value and throw a warning like so:

```
.dTMwMo.MuiDivider-root {
  ⚠ marginTop: "4px";
  ⚠ margin-bottom: "4px";
}
```

This divider was a good candidate for creating a Styled Component because the custom Divider is used multiple times. By creating a Styled Component I specified the style once and didn't need to repeat the CSS.

- **Custom Disabled Accordion**

This example contains a disabled accordion that has a custom color scheme. I researched the classes to target by looking at the Accordion API and confirming with dev tools.

```
//styles
const StyledAccordion = styled(Accordion)`
  &.MuiAccordion-root.Mui-disabled {
    color: purple;
    background-color: teal;
  }
`;

//JSX
<StyledAccordion disabled>
  <AccordionSummary expandIcon={<ExpandMoreIcon
/>}>
    <Typography>Disabled Accordion</Typography>
  </AccordionSummary>
</StyledAccordion>
```

Enabled Accordion	⌄
Disabled Accordion	⌄

- **Custom Fixed AppBar**

This example is an AppBar with position="fixed" property. The position property affects the CSS classes applied in the DOM. Inspect the DOM and see the AppBar API for what classes to target.

```
//styles
const StyledAppBar = withStyles((theme) => ({
  root: {
    backgroundColor:
theme.palette.primary.dark,
    "&.MuiAppBar-positionFixed": {
      "& .MuiToolbar-root": {
        color: "orange",
        "& .MuiButtonBase-root": {
          fontFamily: "Arial"
        }
      }
    }
  }
}))(AppBar);

//JSX
<StyledAppBar
  position="fixed"
  color={"secondary"}
>
  <Toolbar>
    <IconButton
      edge="start"
      className={classes.menuButton}
      color="inherit"
      aria-label="menu"
    >
      <MenuIcon />
    </IconButton>
    <Typography
      variant="h6"
      className={classes.title}
    >
      News
```

```
      </Typography>
      <Button color="inherit">
        Login
      </Button>
    </Toolbar>
  </StyledAppBar>
```

Chapter 3: Material-UI Theming and Additional Resources

A book about styling Material-UI components wouldn't be complete without discussing MUI's custom theming. MUI makes custom theming pretty intuitive. Components then use the custom theme passed to them (or default theme), often without the developer even needing to add any code.

Theme Example:

In the same CodeSandbox used for examples above, I've added a customization to the default MUI theme. Let's take a look at it.

First, I create the custom theme in the file custom-theme.js:

```
export const theme = createMuiTheme({
  status: {
    danger: red[300]
  }
});
```

I've only added one value: status.danger. There are default values that I haven't changed: a suite of *primary*, *secondary*, *error*, *warning*, *info*, and *success* colors. These colors are accessed like this: theme.palette.primary.main and can be modified in the theme if desired. Many components use the primary color suite without the developer needing to specify this in the code. See the documentation on these default colors here: https://material-ui.com/customization/palette/.

Next, I wrap the desired components in the ThemeProvider:

```
<ThemeProvider theme={theme}
  <div className="App">
    <StyledDivider />
```

```
    <CustomFormControl />
    <StyledDivider />
    <CustomDialog />
    <StyledDivider />
    <CustomAccordion />
  </div>
```

In this case I wrapped all the components in the theme provider because this is a small demo app. In a larger production project, you might wrap portions of the app in different ThemeProviders.

Notice how the ThemeProvider accepts a prop 'theme', which is our exported theme from custom-theme.js.

Finally, any component can now access the status.danger color. Take a look at custom-styles.js:

```
export const useStyles = makeStyles((theme) =>
({
  root: {
    "& > *": {
      margin: theme.spacing(2),
      borderColor: theme.status.danger
    }
  }
...
});
```

Notice again the theme prop. Now any component that has access to this useStyles hook can have a border color defined by the custom theme.

The theme can be used to provide global overrides of components. For example, you could style a checkbox in the theme and then it auto-applies to any checkboxes that have been provided that theme. The syntax is below:

```
overrides: {
  MuiButton: {
```

```
    root: {
      "&:hover": {
        backgroundColor: "green"
      }
    }
  }
}
```

Additional Reading and Examples

This book provided a number of Material-UI specific ways of overriding default component styling. Inline styling can also be used when needed. I hope that the methods and examples above will help you create better looking components in less time.

For more free articles on Material-UI customization, visit my blog at https://smartdevpreneur.com/. I cover topics such as styling components, customizing MUI Table, Grid, Button, AppBar, and many more. Listed below are a number of articles on styling components, with code included, that go beyond the scope of this book.

- Material-UI AppBar Color and Styling: https://smartdevpreneur.com/setting-material-ui-appbar-color-and-styling/
- Aligning Buttons in Material-UI Box Component: https://smartdevpreneur.com/align-buttons-in-material-ui-using-the-box-component/
- Implementing Search in Material-UI Table: https://smartdevpreneur.com/the-easiest-way-to-implement-material-ui-table-search/
- Customizing Material-UI Theme Palette: https://smartdevpreneur.com/advanced-theming-customizing-material-ui-theme-palette/
- Customizing Material-UI Table Cell Width: https://smartdevpreneur.com/customizing-material-ui-table-cell-width/
- Material-UI Grid Align Items: https://smartdevpreneur.com/the-complete-guide-to-material-ui-grid-align-items/
- Intro to Material-UI Grid: https://smartdevpreneur.com/intro-to-material-ui-grid-component/

- Intro to Material Table for React: https://smartdevpreneur.com/intro-to-material-table-for-react/

The below resources are links to various documentation on Material-UI.

Additional reading on customizing components:
- Customizing Components: https://material-ui.com/customization/components/
- Advanced Customization: https://material-ui.com/styles/advanced/
- Styles API: https://material-ui.com/styles/api/
- Global Component Overrides: https://material-ui.com/customization/globals/#css
- Class Names: https://material-ui.com/styles/advanced/#class-names

Additional reading on MUI Themes:
- Theming: https://material-ui.com/customization/theming/
- Palettes: https://material-ui.com/customization/palette/
- Colors: https://material-ui.com/customization/color/#examples
- Default Theme Object: https://material-ui.com/customization/default-theme/

www.ingramcontent.com/pod-product-compliance
Lightning Source LLC
LaVergne TN
LVHW041222050326
832903LV00021B/752